PEOPLE AT
THE CENTER OF

THE COLD WAR

By BRITTA BJORNLUND

BLACKBIRCH™
PRESS

THOMSON

GALE

San Diego • Detroit • New York • San Francisco • Cleveland
New Haven, Conn. • Waterville, Maine • London • Munich

THOMSON

GALE

For more information, contact
The Gale Group, Inc.
27500 Drake Rd.
Farmington Hills, MI 48331-3535
Or you can visit our Internet site at http://www.gale.com

Photo credits: cover

page 4, 37 © Wally McNamee/CORBIS; pages 5, 16, 20, 27 © Hulton/Archive - Getty Images; pages 6, 7, 14, 17 © Hulton-Deutsch Collection/CORBIS; pages 8-9, 10, 21, 22, 24, 25, 26, 29, 30, 39, 45 © Bettman/CORBIS; pages 11, 18-19, 23 © CORBIS; pages 12-13 © Robert Maass/CORBIS; page 32 © Bill Gentile/CORBIS; page 33 © Francoise de Mulder/CORBIS; page 34 © Reuters NewMedia Inc./CORBIS; page 38 © William Coupon/CORBIS; page 40 © CORBIS; page 41 © Peter Turnley/CORBIS; pages 42, 43 © Landov;

LIBRARY OF CONGRESS CATALOGING-IN-PUBLICATION DATA

Bjornlund, Britta.
  Cold war / by Britta Bjornlund.
    v. cm. — (People at the center of:)
Includes bibliographical references and index.
Contents: Winston Churchill (1874-1965), British Prime Minister 1940-45, 1951-55 — Kim Il Sung (1912-1994), Premier, North Korea 1948-1994 — Fidel Castro (1926-), leader of Cuba 1959 - present — Leonid Ilyich Brezhnev (1906-1982), General Secretary of the Communist Party of the Soviet Union, 1964-1982, Soviet President 1977-1982.
  ISBN 1-56711-765-1 (hard. : alk. paper)
  1. Cold War. 2. Cold War—Biography. 3. World politics—1945-1989. 4. United States—Foreign relations—Soviet Union. 5. Soviet Union—Foreign relations—United States. [1. Cold War—Biography.] I. Title. II. Series.

  D843.B528 2004
  909.82'5'0922—dc21   2003005428

Printed in United States
10 9 8 7 6 5 4 3 2 1

Contents

THE COLD WAR

Above: The Cold War was essentially a battle both for power and of ideology between the Soviet Union and the United States. Opposite: Americans and Soviets emerged from World War II as world leaders.

The Cold War was a political, military, and diplomatic struggle that defined the last half of the twentieth century. It began at the end of World War II and continued for more than forty-five years until the fall of the Soviet Union in 1991. The Cold War affected people and nations throughout the world but it had two main players: the Soviet Union and the United States. These two superpower countries were engulfed in a battle of ideas, politics, and influence that consumed the globe.

To a certain extent, the Cold War was a power struggle between the two strongest countries in the world. When World War II ended in 1945, the Soviet Union emerged as a major military power. During the war, the Soviet military drove back Nazi Germany's troops from deep within Soviet territory and then moved on to defeat the Nazis in Europe. The United States also emerged from the war as a great world power. Without any fighting on its territory, the United States had been able to create a powerful war economy in which many Americans found solid jobs in the manufacture of arms, machinery, and other goods needed for the war. Many European countries looked toward the United States for assistance in rebuilding their war-torn economies.

The Cold War was also a battle of ideas, a clash between two very different belief systems, or ideologies. The Soviet Union was based on the ideology of communism. Communism promised a classless society where everyone was socially equal and

British prime minister Winston Churchill, U.S. president Franklin D. Roosevelt, and Soviet leader Joseph Stalin (seated left to right) met at Yalta in 1945 to discuss postwar Europe.

where all goods were shared among all people. These ideals were to be maintained by leaders of the Communist Party, the only legal political group, which made most of the decisions for the community. This meant that government and party leaders controlled all aspects of society, including what jobs people held and where they lived. The United States, on the other hand, believed in the ideas of capitalism and democracy. In capitalism, businesses and consumers determine what goods are available in the markets and at what prices. Industries, shops, housing, and land are owned by private individuals. In a democracy, politicians are chosen through open elections. Governmental oversight of everyday life is minimal and allows individuals to make their own decisions.

When the Soviet Union and the United States came together to discuss plans for peace as World War II was coming to an end, they found that their differing ideologies made it difficult to reach agreement. Soviet, American, and British leaders met in 1945 at Yalta (on the Crimean peninsula on the Black Sea) and later that year, after they jointly defeated Nazi Germany, they met again in Potsdam, Germany. Some agreements were made: Germany was to be divided into four occupational zones; the United States, the Soviet Union, Britain, and France would each administer one of the zones. Germany's capital, Berlin, located deep within territory occupied by the Soviet troops, was to be administered by a joint council.

The leaders clashed over many issues, such as the future governments of countries in Eastern Europe. The war had left most parts of Eastern and Central Europe under the control of the Soviet Red Army and the Soviets wanted to keep those areas to protect the Soviet Union from possible future invasions. The British and American leaders, however, wanted to see free elections in Eastern Europe. This dispute was not fully resolved and by the end of 1945, the Soviets had already begun to create pro-Communist governments in many Eastern European countries. U.S. leaders looked at the Soviet expansion with alarm.

Thus the uncertain situation in the world after World War II and the ideological differences between the Eastern European countries and the West set the stage for the Cold War. Although it is called a "cold" war because the Soviet Union and the United States did not directly fight one another in a "hot" conflict, both countries participated on opposite sides in wars in other countries such as Korea, Vietnam, and Afghanistan. In these conflicts, the two

After World War II, Germany was divided into temporary zones governed by four nations. Berlin was also split, and the Berlin Wall became a symbol of the Cold War.

superpowers competed to spread their political views and expand their influence.

The Korean War was the first military confrontation of the Cold War. At the end of World War II, Korea was divided along the thirty-eighth parallel, with the United States influencing the region to the south and the Soviets overseeing the northern part of the country. When the Korean Communists in the north invaded the south in 1950 in an attempt to reunify the country, the United States sent in troops to stop the spread of communism. China and the Soviet Union supported the Korean Communists, and what began as a civil war developed into an international conflict. Fighting came to a close in 1953, with Korea divided at the thirty-eighth parallel to this day.

The next Cold War tragedy was the war in Vietnam. Fighting broke out between the Communist north and the non-Communist south in the mid-1950s. The United States again became involved in the fight against the spread of communism, and slowly committed more and more military to the conflict over the course of more than twenty years. The United States lost thousands of American lives in the brutal fighting before finally pulling out and admitting defeat.

The Vietnam War proved to be a tragic extension of the Cold War.

Afghanistan was another Cold War conflict. In 1978, pro-Communist revolutionaries overthrew the Afghanistan government to establish a new Communist regime. Although the Communist rule was unpopular because of the country's Islamic majority, in December 1979, the Soviet Red Army invaded Afghanistan to install a new Communist leadership. Local Afghan troops fought back and soon the Soviet Union was involved in a drawn-out war. The Soviets pulled out of Afghanistan entirely by February 1989.

Growing tensions between East and West also threatened the world with nuclear destruction. The arms race, in which the United States and the Soviet Union each tried to stockpile more numerous and more powerful nuclear weapons than the other, reached staggering proportions throughout the course of the Cold War. The most glaring example of this threat came to light during the Cuban Missile Crisis. After the failed Bay of Pigs invasion, in which the United States attempted to invade Cuba to depose its Communist dictator, the Soviet Union increased its support of Cuba's Communist regime. In 1962, the Soviet government decided to install medium- and intermediate-range ballistic missiles in Cuba that could reach America in a matter of minutes. The United States responded by starting a naval blockade of Cuba and demanding that the Soviets dismantle the weapons. Misunderstandings and poor

The Soviet Red Army invaded Afghanistan in 1979, and began a decade-long war for control of that country's government.

During the Cuban Missile Crisis, the United States, led by President John F. Kennedy (pictured), opposed the deployment of Soviet missiles in Cuba.

communication created a situation in which for almost two weeks the world stood at the brink of a nuclear disaster. Finally, the Soviets dismantled the weapons and the United States promised never to invade Cuba again and to remove similar U.S. missiles from Turkey, within range of the Soviet Union.

The most striking symbol of the Cold War was the Berlin Wall. Before the wall was built, Berlin had become a major point of tension. In 1949, Germany had split along its eastern and western zones into East Germany, a Soviet-controlled country, and West Germany, a democratic nation that consisted of three zones controlled by Britain, France, and the United States. The city of Berlin was also split between east and west. Located deep within East Germany, West Berlin became the best available escape route for East Germans fleeing Soviet control. To stop the increasing flow of people into the West, the Soviets and East Germans built the Berlin Wall in 1961. East German border guards were ordered to shoot people who tried to escape across the wall. The Berlin Wall separated East and West Berlin for the next twenty-eight years. During this period, the Berlin Wall served as a striking physical reminder of the ideological division between East and West, between communism and capitalism, and between the Soviet Union and the United States.

Cold War tensions seemed to subside during the late 1960s and early 1970s. During this period several arms agreements were reached under a policy known as détente. By the late 1970s and early 1980s, however, Cold War tensions had returned with an acceleration of the arms race and the Soviet invasion of Afghanistan. By 1979 the United States and the Soviet Union had fallen back into a Cold War rivalry. In the mid 1980s, however, sweeping reforms in the Soviet Union led to a decreased Soviet presence in Eastern Europe. Peaceful anti-Communist revolutions swept Eastern and Central Europe in 1989. When the East German government decided to open the Berlin Wall, enthusiastic crowds on both sides of the wall dismantled much of the entire structure in celebration. Two years later, the Soviet Union itself disintegrated. The Cold War had ended.

The changing political climate in the Soviet Union led to the opening of the Berlin Wall (pictured) in 1989.

WINSTON CHURCHILL

Winston Churchill was born on November 30, 1874, in Oxfordshire, England, to a prominent British family. Well schooled, Churchill became a soldier, author, and notable politician. He began his political career in 1900 when he was elected to Parliament, and in 1940, Churchill was named British prime minister.

During World War II, Churchill worked closely with U.S. president Franklin D. Roosevelt to plan the postwar world. He distrusted Soviet leader Joseph Stalin, despite Roosevelt's pleas to cooperate with him. These differences became evident during the Big Three conferences, meetings of Stalin, Roosevelt, and Churchill, in Tehran in 1943 and in Yalta in 1945. During such meetings, Churchill unsuccessfully argued that something must be done to limit Stalin's expansion into Eastern Europe.

Churchill's party lost reelection in 1945 and this caused him to lose his position as prime minister during the Yalta talks. Nonetheless, he continued to be influential in world politics. In 1946, Churchill delivered his famous "Iron Curtain" speech, a significant moment in the beginning phase of the Cold War. Speaking in Fulton, Missouri, Churchill warned of an impending Soviet threat and the inevitability of the division of Europe. His speech seemed to confirm that the world was divided between East and West.

Churchill returned to the position of prime minister in 1951. In his second term he expanded Britain's nuclear program and began Britain's first atom bomb and hydrogen bomb programs. Churchill believed that the buildup or "balance of terror" as he called it would stop the Soviets from expanding their influence throughout the world and preserve the peace. After Stalin's death, Churchill supported meeting with the new leadership in an effort to improve Cold War relations. American policy makers postponed the meeting until 1955, by which time Churchill had already resigned from politics.

In 1953, Churchill was honored by Queen Elizabeth as a Knight of the Garter, Britain's highest order of knighthood. That year, he also won the Nobel Prize in literature for his six-volume *The Second World War*. He suffered a stroke in 1954 and retired in 1955. Churchill died ten years later on January 15, 1965, at the age of 90.

Opposite: Churchill warned there was a threat to postwar Europe from the Soviet Union. In 1946, he coined the term "Iron Curtain" to describe the division of East and West.

Joseph Stalin was born Iosif Vissarionovich Dzhugashvili on December 21, 1879, in the Caucasian region of the Russian Empire known as Georgia. The son of a shoemaker, he became interested in political theory as a student. By 1903, he had joined the Bolshevik party, headed by Vladimir Lenin. In 1912, he changed his last name to Stalin. With Lenin's support, Stalin rose through the Bolshevik ranks and became the general secretary of the Communist Party in 1922.

Above: The Soviets built an atom bomb in 1949. Opposite: Many consider Soviet dictator Joseph Stalin to be the leader most responsible for the Cold War.

After Lenin's death in 1924, Stalin emerged as a powerful dictator who ruled his vast country with terror and cruelty. In the ten years after 1929, Stalin quickly industrialized the Soviet Union at the expense of millions of lives. His forced collectivization of agriculture, in which farmland and assets were transferred into collective or state ownership rather than private ownership, resulted in famine in the 1930s and more than 10 million people died. During the Great Purge, he imprisoned, sent to labor camps, and executed millions of Soviet citizens whom he suspected of opposing his programs. No one was immune from his wrath, and the country lived in a state of suspicion and fear.

After the Nazis invaded Soviet territory in 1941, the Soviet Union joined the allied nations of the United States, Great Britain, and France to end Nazi occupation of the Soviet Union and Europe. Stalin met with U.S. and British leaders at Tehran in 1943 and at Yalta and Potsdam in 1945. Stalin's bargaining position at the meetings was strong, as without the strength of the Soviet Red Army, the Allies might not have won the war. Stalin demanded a buffer zone of friendly territory to protect his country from attack in the future. His insistence on imposing control over Eastern Europe contributed greatly to the Cold War. In fact, Joseph Stalin is thought by many to be the man most responsible for the Cold War.

After learning at Potsdam that the United States had the atomic bomb, Stalin put a priority on developing a Soviet atomic bomb. Soviet scientists achieved this goal in 1949, several years before anyone in the West expected. Stalin also sent aid to Communist regimes in other countries including China and North Korea.

From 1945 until Stalin's death in 1953, the Cold War was at its height, characterized by mutual suspicion and misunderstandings. Stalin remained in power until he died from natural causes at age seventy-three on March 5, 1953.

Stalin made the development of an atomic bomb his scientists' top project after he learned that the United States had already built one.

HARRY S. TRUMAN

SOUGHT TO CONTAIN THE SOVIET THREAT

Harry S. Truman was born on a farm in Missouri on May 8, 1884. After high school he held a variety of jobs before he earned a law degree and entered politics. Truman was elected to the Senate in 1934, and in 1944, during Franklin D. Roosevelt's campaign for a fourth presidential term in office, Truman became Roosevelt's running mate. Truman assumed the position of vice president with little experience in foreign policy and practically no briefings from Roosevelt. When Roosevelt died on April 12, 1945, Truman faced a tremendous challenge because he had little experience with foreign policy.

In July 1945, Truman met with Soviet and British leaders at the Potsdam meetings. Truman took a hard-nosed approach to Stalin and protested the Soviet's interest in Eastern Europe. While at Potsdam, Truman made it clear to the Soviets that the United States had the atomic bomb and thus was now the most powerful country in the world.

When the Soviets blocked ground transport to West Berlin, President Truman ordered food and supplies airlifted to the city.

The period of 1947 to 1949 featured a number of steps under Truman's policy of "containment" that aimed to prevent the Soviets from spreading communism throughout the world. On March 12, 1947, Truman addressed Congress and asked for $400 million in aid for Greece and Turkey. Great Britain was withdrawing economic support to the region and the United States feared that the region might fall to communism. Truman made clear that any threat to peace would now be seen as a security threat to the United States. This policy, known as the Truman Doctrine, promised that the United States would intervene by force if necessary to stop communism from spreading throughout the world.

Truman's policies also included the Marshall Plan that used U.S. resources to stimulate the recovery of European economies outside of the Soviet sphere. In addition, Truman oversaw the Berlin airlift, a military air operation that brought food and supplies to West Berlin after the Soviets tried to blockade that part of the city in an effort to drive out the Western powers, who were collaborating to create a separate West German government in their zones.

In 1947, Truman lobbied Congress for funds to help Greece and Turkey. He felt that such aid would help these countries resist communism.

Under Truman, the United States also participated with eleven Western nations to establish the North Atlantic Treaty Organization (NATO), the first peacetime military alliance. Within a few years, NATO would have fifteen members and would serve as the main military means to contain the Soviets in Europe.

At home, Truman had to deal with the increasing anti-Communist hysteria that implicated members of his administration. In 1948, Truman won reelection to the presidency but his popularity declined during his second term. After this, Truman returned to private life, wrote his memoirs, and created his presidential library. He died at the age of 88 on December 26, 1972.

Born to a poor peasant family on April 15, 1912, Kim Il Sung left Japanese-occupied Korea with his family for Manchuria, in northeastern China, when he was still a small child. In 1941, Kim left Manchuria for the Soviet Far East where he received Soviet military training. By 1945, he had returned to Korea as a major of the Soviet army that liberated North Korea from Japanese occupation. When Soviet troops withdrew from North Korea, he became the first premier of the Communist Democratic People's Republic of Korea. Kim used Soviet support to build up his military and planned to forcibly reunify the country under communism.

In June 1950, Communist North Korean troops under Kim's command and with Soviet approval invaded South Korea. When U.S.-led United Nations troops defeated Kim's armies in South Korea, the United States began a counterattack by advancing troops into the Communist

Opposite: Kim Il Sung trained with the Soviet military and, as premier of North Korea, aimed to unify Korea under communism. Above: Kim's attack on South Korea led to war with UN troops.

North. Kim received assistance from Communist China to drive the UN troops back into South Korea. The conflict that had begun as a civil war among Koreans had developed into an international Cold War battle between Soviet and Chinese Communists and American and Western capitalists. A permanent cease-fire was reached in 1953, and the Korean peninsula was formally divided into two parts, a Communist North Korea under Kim Il Sung, and an anti-Communist South Korea.

After 1953, Kim formed a militarized regime that worshipped him as a deified dictator. Throughout the Cold War, North Korea continued to rely heavily on Soviet and Chinese economic and military support. Kim never accepted the division of his country and continued throughout his life to attempt to overthrow the South Korean government. After the end of the Cold War, in 1993, the United States grew concerned about Kim's nuclear capabilities. The following year, former U.S. president Jimmy Carter convinced Kim to freeze his nuclear program. In return Carter promised to work to ease international sanctions against North Korea. Kim died at the age of 82 on July 8, 1994.

JOSEPH MCCARTHY

TRIED TO EXPOSE AMERICAN COMMUNISTS

Joseph McCarthy was born in Grand Chute, Wisconsin, on November 14, 1908. Although he dropped out of school when he was fourteen, he returned to his studies six years later and received a law degree in 1935. He became a circuit judge in 1940, then served with the U.S. Marines during World War II and achieved the rank of captain. Although McCarthy ran unsuccessfully for the U.S. Senate in 1944, he was elected senator from Wisconsin in 1946.

Most Americans who were accused of being Communists during the McCarthy era could not save their jobs or reputations.

McCarthy's career as a senator was fairly undistinguished until he gave a speech in 1950 in Wheeling, West Virginia, that attracted national attention. McCarthy claimed that more than two hundred Communists had infiltrated the State Department. Although a Senate committee investigated his claim and found it to be fraudulent, McCarthy repeated these allegations in a series of radio and television appearances. In 1953, McCarthy became the chair of the Senate Committee on Governmental Operations, a committee dedicated to investigating waste and illegalities in government. He used his position to continue to exploit Americans' growing fear of communism. In widely publicized hearings, he questioned alleged Communists about their political views and past associations. He presented lists of supposed Communists and recklessly interrogated people at their hearings. Although McCarthy had little to no evidence to support his charges, countless careers were ruined because of these investigations. McCarthy's behavior is the source of the term "McCarthyism," used to describe unfounded witch hunts and fear such as those that dominated that time period.

McCarthy's appeal was proof that the Cold War had taken hold within the United States. McCarthy and other politicians used the fear of communism to further their own aims. McCarthy used it to try to discredit members of the Democratic Party, even high-level officials in the Truman administration. By 1954, however, it was becoming clear that McCarthy's outrageous claims had made him many enemies.

Senator Joseph McCarthy used his power as a senator and Americans' Cold War fear of communism to interrogate alleged Communists and attempt to ruin the reputations of Democratic Party officials.

An investigation of an army major eventually led to his downfall. During live television hearings, army counsel Joseph N. Welsh launched a counterattack that exposed McCarthy's dishonesty. In December 1954, the Senate voted to condemn McCarthy for bringing disrespect to the Senate. McCarthy's influence steadily declined until he died of a liver ailment only a few years later on May 2, 1957.

JOHN FOSTER DULLES

Born in Washington, D.C., on February 25, 1888, John Foster Dulles studied at Princeton University and the Sorbonne in Paris and received a law degree from George Washington University. Dulles had an impressive career in foreign affairs and held key advisory roles at the end of both world wars.

Dulles believed that communism was evil and that the Soviet Union needed to be approached from a position of strength. Named U.S. president Dwight D. Eisenhower's secretary of state in 1953, Dulles crafted the administration's "New Look" policy that redefined the country's military. The New Look policy emphasized minimizing costs by relying on air power and nuclear weapons rather than ground troops and conventional weapons. Dulles criticized the previous policy that tried to contain the Soviet threat, and instead advocated a more aggressive approach to the Soviet Union that included massive retaliation, brinksmanship, and liberation. Massive retaliation promised that the United States would meet any Communist aggression with the nuclear annihilation of the Soviet Union. The overall approach of brinksmanship was that the United States would refuse to back down in the face of a crisis even if it meant going to war. Liberation promised support for countries that were struggling against communism. However, despite this commitment to liberation, when Hungarians rose up against Soviet domination in 1956, the United States did not respond.

Opposite: Secretary of State John Foster Dulles (center) believed in reacting aggressively to the Soviet Union. Above: Despite Dulles's stance, the United States did not help Hungary oust the Soviets in 1956.

Ultimately the Cold War policies pursued by Dulles and the Eisenhower administration led to a further reliance on nuclear weapons. This caused a spiraling arms race between the two superpowers with each country trying to build up more weapons than the other. This atmosphere deepened mistrust and tension between the two countries and intensified the Cold War.

Dulles was diagnosed with terminal cancer in 1958, and he died at the age of 71 on May 24, 1959.

Nikita Sergeyevich Khrushchev was born on April 17, 1894, into a poor Russian peasant family living near the Ukrainian border. In 1908, Khrushchev's family moved to an industrial center in the Ukraine where he began working as a metal fitter in the coal mining industry. Khrushchev was excused from military service because he was a skilled industrial worker and he went on to become a labor activist and a Communist. Khrushchev rose through the Communist Party as a Stalin supporter in the 1920s and 1930s and moved into its top ranks. Appointed to head the Communist Party in the Ukraine during World War II. Khrushchev became one of the key advisers to the Soviet leader, Stalin. After Stalin's death in 1953 and an ensuing two-year power struggle within the Communist Party, Khrushchev emerged as the new Soviet leader.

Khrushchev undertook new reforms in Soviet domestic and foreign affairs that seemed to signal a possible improvement in the Cold War relationship between the United States and the Soviet Union. His early years in power became known as the "thaw" because of the loosening control of the Communist party. In 1956, Khrushchev proved to the world that he was different from his dictatorial predecessor. In a speech to the Communist Party Congress, he denounced Stalin and his reign of terror. During this speech, Khrushchev also spoke about an easing of tensions with the United States.

Despite his intentions to improve relations with the West, several major events during Khrushchev's rule led the Cold War in a different direction. In 1956, during an anti-Communist uprising in Hungary, Khrushchev sent twenty thousand Soviet troops and twenty-five hundred Soviet tanks into the capital city of Budapest in order to forcibly bring the country back under Soviet control. In 1960, the Soviets shot down an American U-2 spy plane flying through Soviet airspace; this incident caused the termination of a Soviet-American summit in Paris and severely soured relations. In 1961, under Khrushchev's leadership, the Soviets helped to construct the Berlin Wall.

In 1962, Khrushchev sent nuclear missiles into the country of Cuba, thus inducing the Cuban Missile Crisis. This crisis brought the world to the brink of nuclear disaster and greatly weakened Khrushchev's reputation among the Communist elite in his country. Two years later he was removed from power.

Khrushchev lived the rest of his days in quiet retirement in rural Russia. He died in 1971.

Nikita Khrushchev initially intended to improve Soviet-Western relations, but instead helped build the Berlin Wall, used force against Hungary, and deployed missiles to Cuba.

JOHN F. KENNEDY

FORCED THE REMOVAL OF SOVIET MISSILES FROM CUBA

John F. Kennedy was born on May 29, 1917, into a wealthy and politically connected Irish Catholic family in Massachusetts. Kennedy was very well schooled at Choate, a private preparatory school, and Harvard University. After serving in the navy during World War II, Kennedy was elected to Congress in 1946 and to the Senate in 1952. Kennedy was elected U.S. president when he narrowly defeated Richard Nixon in 1960.

Once in the White House, Kennedy implemented a "flexible response" policy to contain the Soviets. This policy allowed for an increase in conventional troops (troops that use nonnuclear weapons) as well as the number of nuclear weapons. This military strengthening on all levels would allow the United States to answer any threat. Kennedy's other new initiatives included a program of economic aid to Latin America and the founding of the Peace Corps, a service that sent thousands of Americans to underdeveloped countries to promote economic and social revitalization. Both of these initiatives were attempts to spread the influence of the United States in a peaceful and positive way.

Kennedy suffered several frustrating setbacks in the Cold War, including the crushing defeat at the Bay of Pigs, the construction of the Berlin Wall in 1961, and the Cuban Missile Crisis in 1962. Kennedy has been both praised for his handling of the delicate situation during the Cuban Missile Crisis and criticized for bringing the country to the near edge of nuclear disaster.

Kennedy played a major role in another Cold War tragedy, the Vietnam War. By 1963, the Kennedy administration had significantly increased U.S. support for the anti-Communist but corrupt regime led by Ngo Dinh Diem, and committed more than sixteen thousand military advisers to Vietnam. Kennedy became dissatisfied with Diem, however, and approved a military plot to remove Diem. Kennedy was shocked to learn that the leader had not only been removed by this plot but also assassinated.

Kennedy also oversaw the space race with the Soviet Union. His commitment to winning this competition pushed the United States to land the first man on the moon in 1969. Kennedy was assassinated on November 22, 1963, during a visit to Dallas, Texas.

President John F. Kennedy introduced the Peace Corps and an economic aid program in Latin America as ways to peacefully spread U.S. influence around the world.

FIDEL CASTRO

MADE CUBA A COMMUNIST NATION

Fidel Castro was born on August 13, 1926, in Mayarí, Cuba, to a prosperous farming family. Castro received a law degree in 1950 and was jailed in 1953 for leading a group of guerrillas, called the 26th of July Revolutionary Movement, in a failed takeover of U.S.-supported dictator Fulgencio Batista. After he received amnesty, Castro was exiled from Cuba and lived in Mexico and the United States before returning to his homeland in 1956. Castro successfully ousted Batista in 1959 and took over the island nation.

Because the United States had friendly relations with the Batista regime and had tried to prevent Castro's victory, the new leader was intensely anti-American. Cuba's economy was dominated by American companies, especially in the sugar, telephone, and electricity sectors, and after taking power Castro quickly began seizing American-owned land and property in Cuba. Castro then embraced communism and turned to the Soviet Union for support. Castro angered Americans by breaking trade relations with the United States, signing new agreements with the Soviet Union, taking over American assets, and executing political opponents. This worsening of relations continued in 1960 as many Cubans fled their country to find sanctuary in the United States. In January 1961, just prior to the end of his term, U.S. president Eisenhower broke off diplomatic relations with Cuba.

Above: Many Cubans opposed to Fidel Castro have come to the United States. Opposite: During the Cold War, Castro supported the Soviet Union.

After the United States tried to oust Castro in the failed Bay of Pigs invasion in 1961. Castro aligned himself even closer to his Soviet allies. Less than a year later, the world came to the brink of nuclear annihilation during the Cuban Missile Crisis.

The Cuban Missile crisis led to Castro becoming a well-known and influential leader. For most of the Cold War, the United States boycotted Cuba's economy while the Soviet Union sent massive economic aid. With the fall of the Soviet Union in 1991, Cuba's economy came to near collapse and Castro was forced to implement some reforms that included the expansion of the tourism sector. While the United States government continues to dislike Castro's policies, Castro enjoys some popularity among Cubans. Many Cubans who oppose Castro's regime have fled the country to seek political protection in the United States.

RICHARD NIXON

Richard Milhous Nixon was born on January 9, 1913, in Yorba Linda, California. He attended Whittier College in California and won a scholarship to Duke University Law School in North Carolina where he finished third in his class. Nixon served in the U.S. Navy during World War II.

After the war, Nixon ran for Congress, where he distinguished himself as a staunch anti-Communist. He gained national attention for his role in exposing a state department official, Alger Hiss, as an alleged Soviet spy. In 1950, Nixon was elected to the Senate. Two years later, Nixon was elected vice president under Dwight Eisenhower. After losing a bid for the presidency in 1960, two years later Nixon ran for governor of California and was again defeated.

In 1968, Nixon reentered politics and was elected president. Despite his conservative anti-Communist record while in the U.S. Congress, Nixon sought a more practical approach to the Soviet Union. The policy of détente, developed by Secretary of State Henry Kissinger, favored negotiation and cooperation. Détente was initially successful; the United States and Russia signed a historic arms agreement in Moscow called the Strategic Arms Limitation Treaty, or SALT. This treaty was the first to put limits on antiballistic missile systems (missiles used to intercept offensive missiles) in an attempt to slow down the spiraling arms race. Another highlight of the détente period during Nixon's presidency came during the Conference on Security and Cooperation in Europe held in Helsinki, Finland, in 1974. There, representatives from thirty-five countries formally accepted Soviet border changes that had taken place at the end of World War II.

Nixon was also the first president to visit Communist China. This set the stage for improved U.S.-Chinese relations and U.S. recognition in 1978 of the People's Republic of China. In Vietnam, Nixon oversaw the slow withdrawal of American troops and the eventual end of the war.

Despite his successes in foreign policy, however, Nixon's presidency was severely marred by the Watergate scandal, an incident that exposed corruption in his administration and led to Nixon's resignation in August 1974. After he resigned from office, Nixon wrote books and continued to be involved in foreign affairs. He died on April 22, 1994, at the age of 81.

Although he was strongly anti-Communist, President Nixon was also practical. He favored détente with the Soviet Union and was the first president to visit the People's Republic of China.

LEONID ILYICH BREZHNEV

Leonid Brezhnev was born on December 19, 1906, to a Russian family in the Ukrainian town of Kamensk. Brezhnev joined the Communist Party in 1930 and held a number of local party positions. After the death of Stalin, Brezhnev aligned himself with Nikita Khrushchev, who would go on to become the Soviet leader. By 1964, Brezhnev had become a close assistant to Khrushchev, and from that position he helped to orchestrate Khrushchev's removal from power. After Khrushchev's removal, Brezhnev quickly assumed the post of general secretary of the Communist Party of the Soviet Union in 1964.

Brezhnev's leadership contrasted strongly with that of his predecessor. He gave more power to the Communist Party and the Soviet government, allowing Soviet officials many privileges and benefits. In terms of foreign affairs, Brezhnev was committed to keeping Eastern Europe in the Soviet grip. He sent troops into Czechoslovakia in 1968 to crush the revolutionary "Prague Spring" during which Czechoslovak citizens rose up against Communist control. This gave birth to the Brezhnev doctrine, which asserted Moscow's right to intervene in the affairs of Eastern Europe and other countries to defend socialism.

While keeping a strong hold on Eastern Europe, Brezhnev turned his attention to Cold War affairs. First he oversaw a massive military buildup that brought the Soviet Union on a level footing with the United States, at great expense to the Soviet economy. From this new position of strength, Brezhnev pursued cooperation with the United States. Brezhnev and Nixon met in 1972 to sign the Strategic Arms Limitation Treaty, or SALT, that limited their antiballistic missiles systems (missiles and radars used to intercept offensive missiles).

In 1977, Brezhnev assumed the position of chairman of the Presidium of the Supreme Soviet (a position similar to president), thereby becoming both head of state and head of the Communist Party. He oversaw the acceleration of the arms race, the Soviet invasion of Afghanistan, and a continued deterioration of the Soviet economy in the late 1970s and early 1980s. Brezhnev's health declined in the early 1980s and he died on November 10, 1982, at the age of 75.

As leader of the Communist Party and later of the Soviet Union, Leonid Brezhnev maintained a strong hold on Eastern European nations, sped the arms race, and launched the invasion of Afghanistan.

RONALD REAGAN

CONFRONTED COMMUNIST EXPANSION

Ronald Reagan was born in 1911 in Tampico, Illinois. After graduating from college in 1932, he first worked as a sports announcer. By 1937 he had moved to Hollywood, California, to pursue acting. This was the beginning of a successful career; Reagan acted in more than fifty American movies.

In the late 1940s, Reagan joined a campaign to drive suspected Communists out of the film industry. This was Reagan's first real experience in politics. In 1962, Reagan joined the Republican Party and just four years later he was elected governor of California. Reelected in 1970, he went on to unsuccessfully run for the U.S. presidency in 1976. He won the next presidential election, however, to become the fortieth U.S. president.

During his first term in office, Reagan maintained a strict anti-Communist stance that increased tensions with the Soviets and caused what was termed the "new Cold War." To counter the Soviet threat, the president undertook a massive military buildup, the largest peacetime buildup in U.S. history. Part of this military expansion included plans for the Strategic Defense Initiative (SDI), which envisioned the use of new technology in outer space to defend against missile attack. The Soviets strongly opposed SDI. Reagan exacerbated Cold War tensions when he called the Soviet Union an "evil empire" in a 1983 speech. His first term also saw the birth of the Reagan Doctrine that promised to use military force to oust Communist regimes in developing countries. Under this doctrine, Reagan sent troops to Grenada, Nicaragua, and Afghanistan to fight Communist forces.

Opposite: President Ronald Reagan was a hard-line anti-Communist. Above: Reagan oversaw the largest U.S. military buildup in peacetime, but later signed a treaty with the Soviet Union eliminating some nuclear missiles.

Reagan's second term as president was guided by a much friendlier policy toward the Soviet Union in reaction to the policies of reformer Mikhail Gorbachev, the new Soviet leader. From 1985 to 1988, Reagan and Gorbachev met four times in historic summits. One of the most valuable moments of cooperation came when both signed the Intermediate Nuclear Forces (INF) treaty in 1987. The INF treaty eliminated all intermediate-range nuclear arms held by the United States and Soviets in both Eastern and Western Europe. Nuclear missiles would no longer be pointed at one another in Europe.

After his presidency, Reagan withdrew from the public due to his battle with Alzheimer's disease.

MIKHAIL GORBACHEV

MADE REFORMS THAT LED TO THE SOVIET UNION'S COLLAPSE

Mikhail Gorbachev was born on March 2, 1931, not far from the city of Stavropol in southern Russia. In 1951, he joined the Communist Party. He graduated from Moscow State University with a law degree in 1952 but returned to Stavropol in the early 1960s to work for the regional party committee. Elected to the Communist Party's central committee in 1971, Gorbachev became a full member of the politburo, the upper ranks of the party and ruling governmental committee, in 1980.

In 1985, Gorbachev was chosen as general secretary of the Communist Party of the Soviet Union. In this position he undertook economic and political reforms, known as perestroika and glasnost, which were unprecedented in the Soviet Union. Perestroika called for a full restructuring and revitalization of the economy, and glasnost allowed for an opening up of society through relaxed controls on information and decreased censorship. Gorbachev also aggressively pursued plans to stop the arms race with the United States.

Because of both his reforms at home and his new thinking in foreign policy, Mikhail Gorbachev is probably the man most responsible for ending the Cold War. One year after signing the Intermediate Nuclear Forces (INF) treaty in 1987 to remove all intermediate-range nuclear missiles from Europe, Gorbachev announced that the Soviet Union would withdraw from Afghanistan. Later that year in a speech to the United Nations General Assembly, Gorbachev declared that the Soviets would reduce their armed forces in Eastern Europe. This set the stage for revolutions against communism to break out throughout Eastern Europe. Gorbachev did not intervene to save communism in Eastern Europe or to reinstitute Soviet control; instead, he let communism dissolve.

Soviet leader Mikhail Gorbachev brought liberating reforms to his country in the 1980s.

Gorbachev (right) worked with President George H.W. Bush (left) to end the arms race. Gorbachev's withdrawal of Soviet troops from Afghanistan and other efforts toward peace were instrumental in ending the Cold War.

At home, Gorbachev's reforms produced a momentum for real change—change that led to the total collapse of the Soviet Union in 1991. Known in the West as "Gorby," he was *Time* magazine's Man of the Year in 1987 and its Man of the Decade for the 1980s. Gorbachev won the Nobel Peace Prize in 1990. He still lives in Russia and remains active in international affairs.

LECH WALESA

Born in 1943 in Popowo, Poland, Lech Walesa was the son of a carpenter. He became an electrical engineer in the Lenin Shipyard in Gdańsk, Poland, in 1967. A political activist, in 1970, Walesa participated in mass demonstrations at the shipyard against rising food prices and was later fired because of his protests. Walesa was arrested many times between 1976 and 1980 for his protest activities.

Elected president of Poland in 1989, Lech Walesa had a history of political activism and was the first person in Eastern Europe to successfully oppose communism there.

Walesa's role in dealing with the Communists to gain greater political freedoms in Poland won him international recognition and Western praise. Walesa became the head of Solidarity, the first independent labor union in the history of Communist Eastern Europe. In 1981, the Polish government disbanded Solidarity and arrested Walesa.

Released in 1982, Walesa went on to win the Nobel Peace Prize in 1983, much to the embarrassment of the Polish government. He continued to agitate for reform, and was instrumental in bringing about the "roundtable talks" in February 1989 between Solidarity and the Communist government. As a result of the talks, Solidarity became a legal movement that was allowed to run candidates for election to the parliament. Solidarity captured ninety-nine of one hundred seats in the senate in the June elections and a majority of seats in the lower house.

Walesa was crucial to the melting of the Cold War, as he was the first to successfully stand up against communism in Eastern Europe. His leadership and courage against communism in Poland set an example for other countries in the

*As leader of Solidarity, the first independent labor union in Eastern Europe,
Walesa spoke out against the Poland's Communist government.*

Soviet bloc. In 1989 massive demonstrations broke out throughout Eastern Europe
as people called for Communist leaders to step down. These revolutions and the
dismantling of the Berlin Wall in 1989 promised the end of the Cold War.

Walesa was elected president of Poland in 1989. Walesa lost his reelection
campaign in 1995. He still remains active in Polish politics.

◎ CHRONOLOGY

February 1945	Churchill, Roosevelt, and Stalin meet at Yalta Conference.
July 1945	Truman, Stalin, and Churchill meet at Potsdam Conference.
1946	Churchill delivers "Iron Curtain" speech in Fulton, Missouri.
1947	Truman outlines anti-Communist policy that becomes known as the Truman Doctrine. Secretary of State George Marshall proposes Marshall Plan, a recovery program for Europe financed by the United States.
1948	Soviet Union stops all land traffic to West Berlin, which begins the Berlin Blockade.
1949	North Atlantic Treaty Organization (NATO) is founded. Soviets develop atomic bomb.
1950	McCarthy gives speech in Wheeling, West Virginia, about presence of Communists in the State Department. Korean War begins.
1953	Joseph Stalin dies. Eisenhower administration begins "New Look" policy.
1956	Nikita Khrushchev denounces Stalin and his crimes in a speech. Khrushchev sends troops and tanks to crush rebellion in Hungary.
1959	Fidel Castro ousts Fulgencio Batista; takes over the rule of Cuba.
1960	Soviets shoot down American U-2 spy plane in Soviet airspace.
1961	United States breaks diplomatic ties with Cuba. The Bay of Pigs invasion fails. United States sends its first military advisers into Vietnam. Berlin Wall is erected as a barricade between East and West Berlin.
1962	Cuban Missile Crisis begins.
1964	Khrushchev is ousted from power; Leonid Brezhnev becomes new Soviet leader.
1968	Troops enter Czechoslovakia to end reforms known as the Prague Spring.

The Berlin Wall (pictured) stood for twenty-eight years. It was dismantled two years before the end of the Cold War.

1969	Era of détente begins. Strategic Arms Limitation Treaty (SALT) talks between the United States and the Soviet Union begin.
1972	Nixon travels to China.
1974	During Conference on Security and Cooperation in Europe (CSCE) held in Helsinki, Finland, representatives from thirty-five countries formally accept Soviet border changes that had taken place at the end of World War II.
1979	United States formally recognizes China. Soviet troops enter Afghanistan.
1983	In a speech, President Reagan calls the Soviet Union an "evil empire." Reagan announces plans to develop the Strategic Defense Initiative (SDI).
1985	Mikhail Gorbachev is chosen as the new general secretary of the Communist Party of the Soviet Union.
1987	Gorbachev and Reagan sign Intermediate Nuclear Forces (INF) treaty.
1989	Soviet troops leave Afghanistan. Roundtable talks begin in Poland. Throughout Eastern Europe, nations rebel against Communist rule. Berlin Wall comes down.
1991	The Soviet Union disbands.

⊚ FOR FURTHER INFORMATION

BOOKS

Michael G. Kort, *The Cold War*. Brookfield, CT: Millbrook, 1994.

Michael Kort, *Mikhail Gorbachev*. New York: Franklin Watts, 1990.

John Pimlott, *The Cold War: Conflict in the 20th Century*. New York: Franklin Watts, 1987.

James A. Warren, *Cold War: The American Crusade Against World Communism, 1945–91*. New York: Lothrop, Lee, & Shepard, 1996.

WEBSITES

CNN Interactive Site on the Cold War
www.cnn.com/specials/cold war
Created to complement the CNN Cold War documentary series, this site contains the documentary's script, as well as a knowledge bank, a debate and discussion area, articles and documents from the period, interviews, and an interactive game. A great resource.

The Cold War Museum
www.coldwar.org
This site includes a time line with good reference materials, online exhibits, games, and a spy tour.

20th Century History Website
http://history1900s.about.com
A website for kids that includes major events, maps, people, and time lines. Many Cold War topics and biographies can be found.

Britta Bjornlund's keen interest in the relationship between the Soviet Union and the United States originated in high school when she began learning Russian and traveled to the Soviet Union for the first time. Currently a program manager at the Center for Russian Leadership Development at the Library of Congress, she holds a master's degree in international relations from the Johns Hopkins University School of Advanced International Studies and a bachelor's degree from Williams College. Ms. Bjornlund has worked as an adviser to various government agencies throughout the former Soviet Union, and she witnessed the fall of the USSR firsthand in 1991. She lives in Washington, D.C., with her cat Trotsky, and is an avid fan of the Washington Capitals ice hockey team.